LITTLE BOOK OF

FENDI

For Rupert Juan

This book is a publication of Welbeck Non-Fiction Limited, part of Welbeck
Publishing Group Limited and has not been licensed, approved, sponsored,
or endorsed by any person or entity. Any trademark, company name, brand
name, registered name and logo are the property of their respected owners
and used in this book for reference and review purpose only.

Published in 2024 by Welbeck
An imprint of the Welbeck Publishing Group
Offices in: London – 20 Mortimer Street, London W1T 3JW &
Sydney – Level 17, 207 Kent St, Sydney NSW 2000 Australia
www.welbeckpublishing.com

A CIP catalogue for this book is available from the British Library.

ISBN 978-1-80279-653-7

Printed in China

10 9 8 7 6 5 4 3 2 1

LITTLE BOOK OF

FENDI

The story of the iconic fashion house

LAIA FARRAN GRAVES

WELBECK

CONTENTS

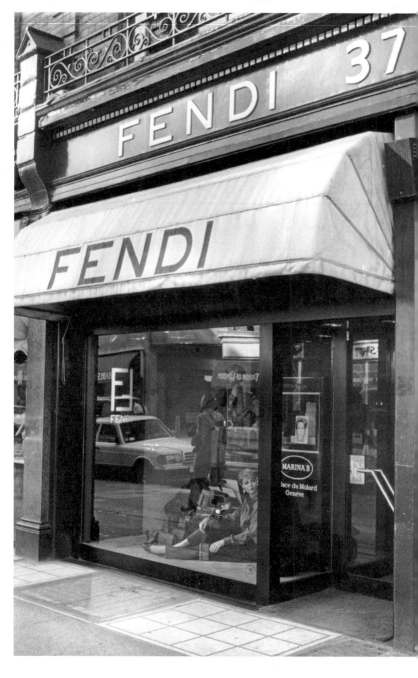

IN THE
BEGINNING

The *Little Book of Fendi* is the story of one of
Italy's finest and most celebrated luxury brands.
Founded in Rome in 1925 by Adele Casagrande
and Edoardo Fendi, it began as a modest leather
and fur shop in Via del Plebiscito, with an atelier
and living quarters above the store.

The brand soon became known for its attention to detail
and love of craftsmanship – with lines such as the
Selleria bag collection, which was completely hand-
sewn. Their growing success enabled the business to expand and
to move premises to the up-and-coming neighbourhood of the
Via Piave. The couple had five daughters – Paola, Franca, Alda,
Anna and Carla – all of whom ended up working in different
capacities for the family firm in perfect harmony, making it the
perfect family business.

OPPOSITE The unmistakable Fendi shopfront of one of its early London stores.

OPPOSITE A
collaboration
between Fendi and
Fila is displayed in
an exhibition at the
Bundeskunsthalle,
Bonn, Germany,
in 2021.

A new era for the fashion house began during the Dolce Vita period – the years of economic boom celebrated by the famous film – and in 1964 Fendi opened a larger store on the prestigious Via Borgognona, where they dressed glamorous Italian film stars, including Claudia Cardinale and Sophia Loren. Fendi was the one to watch and, in 1965, the Fendi sisters made a bold move and took the decision to recruit a young German designer to work as their creative director: the one and only Karl Lagerfeld – a partnership so successful that he held the position for over 54 years, until his death in 2019.

During his time at Fendi Lagerfeld designed the double F logo, which stood for Fun Furs, and went on to elevate the brand's overall status by redefining fur and making it accessible to a wider audience. He also staged the most extraordinary and ingenious fashion shows, including a Spring/Summer 2008 collection that took place at the Great Wall of China, Fendi's first Haute Fourrure (Haute Fur) in Autumn/Winter 2015, and their Autumn/Winter 2016 show, the house's second couture collection, presented at Rome's Trevi Fountain (which was covered in plexiglass for the occasion to create a dramatic catwalk over the water).

Following Lagerfeld's death, British designer Kim Jones was warmly welcomed into the Fendi clan. He was hired as creative director for womenswear in September 2020, and his fresh approach has, once again, repositioned the brand and made it relevant, while maintaining its desirability and staying true to its Roman roots. He introduced the first Fendi Spring/Summer couture collection in a star-studded debut show, which was a stunning interpretation of Virginia Woolf's book *Orlando: A Biography*, and then marked the Baguette's 25th anniversary (Fendi Resort 2023) with a show where Fendi collaborated with Tiffany & Co. and Marc Jacobs.

Today, Fendi has transcended the world of fashion and has become firmly embedded in popular culture. The Fendi Baguette, for example, designed by Silvia Venturini Fendi in 1997, was popularized by Sarah Jessica Parker in the acclaimed TV series *Sex and the City* (1998–2004), marking the birth of the "It" bag phenomenon. Fendi is also loved by celebrities, seen in films, mentioned in music, and its collaborations and advertising campaigns have become as iconic as the pieces themselves. This is the story of a once small Italian family business that conquered the fashion world.

OVERLEAF Fendi's supersized flagship store in Tokyo, Japan, echoes the Fendi headquarters, Palazzo della Civiltà Italiana in Rome. It sells women's and men's collections and has a VIP room reserved for exclusive customers.

THE EARLY
YEARS

F IS FOR FAMILY

"Artisanal savoir-faire, luxury and contemporary design" – Fendi.com

The famed Italian luxury house Fendi – synonymous with classic, luxurious elegance and quality – began as a small family-run business, deeply rooted in the Eternal City of Rome. The metropolis, described by Silvia Venturini Fendi (Creative Director of Accessories and Menswear) as an open-air museum, has provided the house with a constant source of inspiration, bringing together traditional craftsmanship techniques and modern ideas. As such, the word "Roma" is sometimes added to the brand's logo, reinforcing their love for the capital. Today, Fendi produces exquisite ready-to-wear collections for men and women, leather goods and fur, fragrances and accessories – including shoes, eyewear and watches. It also has a homeware line (Fendi Casa was launched

OPPOSITE Italian furs and leather group company Fendi. The five Fendi sisters are left to right: Alda, Paola, Anna, Carla and Franca.

in 1989) and a children's collection (Fendi Kids, from Spring/Summer 2011), all of which are available online or in one of their 200+ stores worldwide.

The Fendi story begins with Adele Casagrande, a talented designer of leather goods and an entrepreneur who was very much ahead of her time. She opened a workshop in 1918, and founded Fendi when she married Edoardo Fendi, the son of a lady-in-waiting to Queen Margherita of Savoy. Adele was stylish and skilful with a great eye for fashion, and Edoardo was a visionary who had an unwavering belief in the brand's success. The couple married in 1925, and the following year opened their first leather and fur store in Rome's central Via del Plebiscito, complete with an on-site workshop and living quarters above the outlet.

The premium quality of the materials procured was central to their success, as was their creative and experimental approach. They worked with talented artisans and combined specialist classic techniques with new ones to achieve stunning finishes and unique results. In 1932, they created a line of leather goods and luggage called the Selleria ("saddlery" in Italian), inspired by noblemen's carriages that travelled past their shop on their way to the seaside, complete with exquisite hand-crafted equestrian leather bridles and other equipment. The Selleria masterpieces were assembled and stitched entirely by hand, employing the same ancient methods that had been used by Roman master saddlers, and were made with *cuoio* Romano, premier soft, grainy Roman leather. This iconic collection – Fendi's first handbag series – became popular for its simplicity and meticulous savoir faire (it took up to six times longer to create a hand-cut and stitched Selleria bag than a machine-made counterpart). It also encapsulated the house's determination to combine craftsmanship and tradition with a contemporary aesthetic.

The brand grew and became known for its exceptional workmanship, and that same year Fendi moved premises to the up-and-coming neighbourhood of the Via Piave. The following year, 1933, they launched their signature *Pergamena* (parchment) leather, a distinct yellowed processed skin that became synonymous with the house and was used frequently in their luggage collections. Reminiscent of Rome's ancient historical monuments, these skins were traditionally dried without tanning, then oiled, greased and smoothed.

The Fendis went on to have five daughters, and gave all of them short names, which suited their surname: Paola, Anna,

Franca, Carla and Alda. They enjoyed learning from their mother about the business from an early age (as babies they were tucked into the handbag drawer for a nap!) and once they'd completed their studies they decided, one by one, to join the family firm, to which they became utterly dedicated. They carved out their own roles within the organization based on their personal strengths: Paola, the eldest, started to work in the HQ at Via Piave when she was just 15, and in time became an expert in fur. She took part in international fur auctions, experimented with techniques, developed new tanning processes and oversaw the dyes. Anna was made executive director of the bags and leather goods department – she created a pleating technique with ribbon and leather which was used on bags in their very first fashion show, Amore (1950), in Rome's Grand Hotel. She was also to be in charge of design and licensing. Franca became store manager and later purchasing manager as well as taking care of accessories. Carla was head of marketing and had a natural flair and understanding for public relations – over time she became the brand's public face. And, finally, Alda began working in the fur atelier and later became its manager. Soon, they were all working dynamically together, fearlessly creating new shapes and tenaciously embracing the future, always united when making important decisions. Their mother Adele would tell them lovingly: "You are like the five fingers of the hand."

OPPOSITE Fendi created new silhouettes that made fur accessible to a wider audience, as in this Autumn/Winter 1983 full-length coat.

"We are not doing basic mink coats, we are a thousand miles away from that."

– Karl Lagerfeld

During the 1940s and the early 1950s, the family worked hard to establish their identity on the Italian fashion scene, with creative energy and plenty of ideas, and shortly after Mr Fendi died, in 1960, his daughters – the next generation – were fully in charge. With an economic boom as a backdrop, Italy's *Dolce Vita* era – coined after Fellini's 1960 film – was a golden time for Italian premier fashion brands. Hollywood had fallen in love with the lifestyle set out in *Roman Holiday* (1953), starring Audrey Hepburn and Gregory Peck: oversized sunglasses, expressos, Vespas, and all things Made in Italy were very much *alla moda*. The House of Fendi was flourishing and expanding, and, in 1964, opened a larger store on the prestigious Via Borgognona. Fendi furs were now dressing Italian stars, including Claudia Cardinale and Sophia Loren.

But despite having strong individual personalities, the Fendi sisters shared a clear vision for the house's future and, as advised by PR Director Franco Savorelli di Lauriano, decided it was time to recruit a fresh young designer then freelancing for several brands including Chloé: the great Karl Lagerfeld. They travelled to Paris to meet him, with an agreement for him to sign, but apparently, when they reached his apartment, there was nobody there. They took it in turns to press the communal hallway lights while they waited and eventually, three hours later, he arrived. The girls and their newly appointed designer were a match made in heaven: the German designer began a collaboration with Fendi in 1965 (on a freelance basis, sometimes working remotely, which at the time was a ground-breaking concept), and the rest, as they say, is history. On his first day working for Fendi, Lagerfeld was wearing a Cerruti hat over his long hair, dark glasses, a printed Ascot tie, a tweed Norfolk jacket, French-style culottes, boots and a large bag purchased in Milan. He was ready to rewrite fashion history.

OPPOSITE Karl Lagerfeld's work with leather was revolutionary. His Autumn/Winter 1981 collection included intricate detailing of fur trimming.

OVERLEAF Karl Lagerfeld, Fendi's creative director for Fur and women's ready-to-wear, sits with the Fendi sisters. From left to right: Franca, Paola, Carla, Alda and Anna.

ABOVE A portrait of French-born Italian actress Catherine Spaak, with Fendi travelling bags, which featured in *Vogue* April 15, 1972.

At the sisters' request, and understanding the importance of having a trademark, he designed the legendary double F Fendi logo, which he drew in all of three seconds and which stood for *Fun Furs*. The monogram print, referred to by Fendi as the *Zucca* (and *Zucchino* for the smaller version), was originally intended to line garments, but in time it took over the house's identity, replacing the 1925 logo of a squirrel (Eduardo would say of Adele that she was as busy as a squirrel). It became integral to the brand's DNA, and central to its success when logomania took off in the 1990s.

Karl Lagerfeld worked with the house for over 50 uninterrupted years, the longest partnership of its kind in the fashion world – referred to as fashion's longest love story – and was instrumental in turning the fur industry landscape on its head. Together, they revolutionized the market and redefined fur: no longer a bourgeois status symbol, it was now considered stylish, elegant and wearable, the ultimate luxe fashion statement. Despite their manufacturer's objections, but with their mother's full blessing, the Fendi sisters had already developed new techniques to make coats much more fluid and light, removing some of the lining and crinolines (previously up to five layers of protective fabric was the norm).

The 1960s and '70s continued to be a time of expansion for Fendi, which was now branching out into ready-to-wear collections and accessories. In their workshop, sometimes referred to as a laboratory, fur was transformed – altered, manipulated and reinterpreted in unprecedented ways. Lagerfeld and the Fendi sisters were always experimenting with patterns, colours and finishes to create something new and fashionable. The fur was also weaved and knitted, pleated, carefully deconstructed and pieced back together, shaved and dyed. Later, it was even embellished with beading, embroidery, silver (for the Autumn/Winter 2015 couture show) and 24-carat gold (for Autumn/Winter 2008, when the fur was deposited into a molecular chamber that added gold particles onto the garment). Eventually, Lagerfeld used other natural materials like chiffon, cashmere and wool to mimic fur – the ultimate irony.

Lagerfeld's work quickly opened the door to an international audience, in particular to the United States, and in 1968 Fendi took hold of the American market. Anna and Carla arrived in the US with trunks of fur, which were bought entirely by Henri Bendel, the New York women's department store.

OVERLEAF
Lagerfeld's Spring/ Summer 1983 presentation highlighted femininity in a collection that included white looks accessorized with gloves.

Bloomingdales was next in line to purchase from Fendi, with a particular interest in their bags, and also presented the first Fendi fragrance to the US market in 1987. Another American luxury department store, Bergdorf Goodman, reserved a dedicated space to Fendi in 1976 and displayed their goods in both windows of their legendary Fifth Avenue entrance.

The Fendis also worked with some of Italy's most influential film-makers – including Luchino Visconti and Federico Fellini – and dressed actresses and international celebrities such as Diana Ross, Catherine Deneuve and Grace Jones. In 1977 Fendi's first ready-to-wear collection was launched, but instead of presenting it as a traditional catwalk show, an 18-minute short film was made, the first of its kind. Directed by Jacques de Bascher, *Histoire d'Eau* stars model Suzy Dyson as a young heiress in Rome (and not at the baths of Germany's Baden-Baden, as she had promised her mother). Modelling the entire collection (from swimsuits to coats), she strolls through the city, splashing in the legendary fountains and collecting their precious water in glass containers. She is also seen relaxing in her hotel room. In the film, she receives an invitation from the Fendi sisters to try on five fur coats, which await her in an empty room resembling a photographic mirrored studio. Then there's a phone call from Carla Fendi asking her to dine with them at their busy atelier, where Carla, Anna and her daughter Maria Teresa and Silvia Fendi make a cameo appearance.

When Adele passed away, in 1978, the Fendi sisters inherited the ownership of the company, each acquiring a 20 per cent share with Paola as their president. In their office hung a framed picture of their matriarch and beloved *mamma*, Adele never to be forgotten.

In 1985, Fendi celebrated its 60th birthday. The occasion was marked with an art exhibition held in Rome's National Gallery of Modern Art, called *Fendi and Karl Lagerfeld:*

Un Percorso di Lavoro (*Fendi and Karl Lagerfeld: A Working Path*); that year they also designed the uniforms for Rome's police department. Three years later, in London in 1988, the brand featured in all 26 windows of Harrods, Knightsbridge's acclaimed luxury department store. This was a first, and it positioned them firmly in the top ranking of the fashion world. In 1989 they opened their first US store in New York's Fifth Avenue.

The millennium brought further changes: in 1999 Fendi was bought by Prada and LVMH (the Louis Vuitton Moët-Hennessy group), with LVMH chairman and CEO Bernard Arnault in charge, and when Prada sold its share in 2001, LVMH became the major shareholder, gradually acquiring the rest of the family's remaining shares. The takeover by a French corporation took the label to the next level, transforming Fendi into a multinational brand while at the same time retaining – perhaps even deepening – its beloved Roman roots: their

LEFT A Fendi store in the heart of Florence, Italy.

production in Florence was doubled and a new shoe factory was opened in the Marche region.

To celebrate their 90th anniversary (and Lagerfeld's 50th year working with the brand), Fendi moved headquarters. They can now be found in the neoclassical Palazzo della Civiltà Italiana, also known as the Square Colosseum, a controversial building that combines old and new, commissioned in 1943 by dictator Benito Mussolini. The space, which underwent an 18-month renovation, is clad in striking white travertine marble. It has 54 imposing arches (distributed across six galleries of nine openings), under which, on the ground floor, stand 28 statues representing different industries. The building, spacious enough to accommodate Fendi's 450 employees, hosts a permanent gallery on the ground floor which is open to the general public.

The following year, 2016, the seventeenth-century Palazzo Fendi on Largo Carlo Goldoni street became Fendi's permanent flagship store in Rome. The almost 10,800 square feet building, a stone's throw away from the Spanish Steps, has five floors. On the ground floor you can shop in the stunning boutique, with its classical interior and contrasting modern bronze and glass lift taking centre stage – like the brand itself, forever combining old and new. The second floor, or Palazzo Privé, is an exclusive, luxurious space, designed by Dimore Studio and reserved to host VIP clients, celebrities and friends of the brand. This beautifully curated apartment has a large foyer, dining room and lounge, as well as a fitting room, and merges vintage antique pieces with contemporary art and design. On the third floor there are seven very elegant modern and exclusive hotel suites, and the top two floors are home to the acclaimed contemporary Japanese restaurant and cocktail bar Zuma, where you can sip on a saké – or perhaps a Campari – while enjoying panoramic views of the legendary city.

OPPOSITE Fendi's elegance is encapsulated in this beautiful leather bag, featured in the Spring/Summer 2020 show.

OVERLEAF With Karl Lagerfeld as creative director, Fendi transformed fur using innovative techniques, such as gilding it with 24-carat gold, seen in this Autumn/Winter 2008 collection.

THE SIXTH
FENDI CHILD

THE
LAGERFELD YEARS

**"Fendi is my Italian version of creativity.
It's Italian to its core. It's not only Italian,
it's Roman" – Karl Lagerfeld**

In 1965 Karl Lagerfeld was welcomed into the Fendi family. The avant-garde designer was hired as Creative Director of fur to add a "young touch" to their fur collection, in a unique relationship that was to last over 54 years. "I should be in the *Guinness Book of Records*," he told *The CNBC Conversation*. Lagerfeld loved to draw and to tell stories through his designs. He always had a notepad and some pens and coloured crayons to hand, ready to draft fashion designs and technical drawings. It is said that during the fittings he worked with the *première* (head of the atelier) with a sketch in hand, comparing it to the garment and making remarks such as "I'm sorry, but it's a millimetre off just there…" And while he disposed of many sketches – describing the wastepaper

OPPOSITE Karl Lagerfeld, seen here sporting his trademark large sunglasses, was often affectionately referred to as the Kaiser of Fashion because of his German roots.

basket as the most important piece of furniture in one's
home – he produced over 70,000 exquisite freehand
sketches and drawings during his time at Fendi, true
masterpieces that are safely kept in Fendi's archive.

He worked closely with the Fendi sisters to define the
fashion house's unmistakable identity, combining beauty
with a confident and fearless attitude. Together, they also
transformed and challenged the world's perception of fur,
taking it from bourgeois, ho-hum status symbol to – as
per Lagerfeld's double F logo – fun fur. Lagerfeld, whose
objective was to challenge the way this material was used,
created the first ready-to-wear Fendi collection in 1977 and
became Head of Womenswear. The collection combined
off-the-peg garments with fur and was presented in ground-
breaking form: the first fashion film, entitled *Histoire d'Eau*.
This was the first of many interpretations of the house's style
– sometimes minimal, sometimes opulent but always cool,
elegant, contemporary and luxurious.

In 1978 Lagerfeld designed a collection of shoes, and
season after season continued to experiment with leather
goods and fur, which for the first time was treated as any
other fabric. New finishes were created, challenging technical
boundaries with the help of a unique team of superior Italian
artisan masters and their traditional expertise. During the
1950s Fendi had already woven velvet and grosgrain ribbons
with fur to create a lighter material with a linear pattern.
Then, in 1966, fur was dyed and coloured for the first time,
broadening the spectrum of colours in which it was normally
available. During the 1970s a practice called *Tegole* (tile in
Italian) was developed, consisting of cutting up the fur is small
sections and overlapping it, like a tiled roof. New textures were
explored with shaving techniques that produced geometric
patterns and gradient lengths. Hand-embellished fur with

beads and sequins, and feathered fur that combined both materials, were also inimitable, with breath-taking finishes patiently developed in the Fendi ateliers. This extraordinary level of craftsmanship was recognized in 1985, when Rome's National Gallery of Modern Art featured Fendi's work in its first-ever fashion exhibition.

But Fendi's progression didn't stop there and the fashion house expanded rapidly into other markets: that same year, 1985, it launched its first fragrance, *Fendi for Women*, followed in 1987 by the sportswear and accessories collection *Fendissime*, led by Silvia Venturini Fendi. *Fendi Uomo*, a men's fragrance, came out in 1988, also the year Fendi Casa (homewear) began. More scents were produced during the 1990s and the 2000s in association with LVMH and with the aid of the finest perfumers in the industry, including Olivia Giacobetti, Jean Guichard and Christine Nagel. Fendi's menswear collections were introduced in the early 1990s and, in 2011, Fendi Kids was created.

Fendi's symbiotic relationship with the arts and entertainment world is present throughout its journey. Music, for instance, is integral to Fendi's presentations and has been performed either on stage (such as the Chinese singer Jackson Wang performing "Fendiman" for Autumn/Winter 2019), or composed specifically for Fendi shows (e.g. Alessandro Cortini's original composition for Menswear Spring/Summer 2022). From the outset, the house has presented collections in unexpected locations and exceptional settings: an early example is the Spring/Summer 1982 show. This collection, themed *Art and Fashion*, took place during the Moda Italiana convention, and was a static show complete with suspended mannequins, in a 150-square metre (1,600-square foot) space at the Fiera Milano exhibition centre.

Another surprising setting was the 1986 presentation on the city's Spanish Steps, to mark the end of Rome's Fashion

Week, which was televised as part of the first episode of a Rai3 TV entertainment programme called *Donna sotto le stelle* (Women Under the Stars, 1986–2003). Always looking to the future, Fendi was also the first fashion label to use camera drones in their shows (Autumn/Winter 2014), enabling them to live-stream on their website and social media platforms to their many followers. The show opened and closed with Cara Delevingne, who wore a classic black fur-hooded belted coat with white boots. With a glint in her eye, she was holding a *Karlito* keychain bag charm: the accessory, made to resemble Lagerfeld, was made of fox fur and mink, cost $1,750 and had a designated waiting list.

In 1992, Silvia Venturini Fendi, who first met Lagerfeld when she was just four years old, was invited by both him and her mother, Anna Fendi, to join them at the main creative studio. Her career at Fendi had started as a child, modelling the Autumn/Winter 1967–68 unisex collection, and she understood the business inside out. "She is there not because she is a Fendi but because she is good," insisted Lagerfeld. Her energy and greater involvement – she became Head of Accessories and of Menswear two years later – strengthened the Fendi DNA, which remained embodied in all their collections, despite their acquisition in 2001 by LVMH's Bernard Arnault. The legacy lives on in the Fendi dynasty, with designer Delfina Delettrez, Silvia's daughter and a fourth generation Fendi, becoming the house's Artistic Director of Jewellery in 2020.

RIGHT A beautiful handcrafted Fendi handbag with a geometric pattern reminiscent of Art Deco design.

OPPOSITE A model walks down the catwalk for Autumn/ Winter 2016, wearing a short coat with coloured stripes set into the fur.

"I use everything from the past and everything from the present so I can make something for the future"
– Karl Lagerfeld in conversation with *Vogue*

Fendi Spring/Summer 2000 was described by *Vogue* as one of Lagerfeld's strongest collections of the season. It was a delicate and colourful exhibit of pencil skirts and cocktail dresses in bright colours – yellow, lime, pink, peach – with lots of sheer chiffon and interesting combinations such as patent leather with a lace finish. Accessories were also key in this collection – from a snakeskin Baguette handbag and bright generous totes, to open-toe boots and metallic high heels. Floral shorts and aviator glasses completed this eclectic, timeless look. The Autumn/Winter 2000 collection that followed was opulent and glamorous, alluding to a '60s fashion silhouette: A-line dresses and skirts nipped at the waist, long leather boots, optical prints, patent leather jackets and belted coats, all of which came together in muted tones.

In contrast, Spring/Summer 2002 told a very different story: gladiator boots, boho accessories and layered outfits in mostly black, brown and red were central to a show with models reminiscent of urban warriors (their hair was mostly braided, and make-up was made to look like a long tattoo across the eyes). Delicate brown leather flowers added a touch of softness, worn on chokers, at the waist and as traditional decorative corsages. Autumn/Winter 2002 was another display of technical brilliance in a true Fendi show, complete with full-length looks, fur capes, coats, long leather boots

and embellished handbags. "We cut the fur to shreds and then knitted it to treat it like a fabric to give it lightness and movement," commented Lagerfeld to *Vogue*. In the Autumn/Winter 2005 collection, more experimental finishes were on display: coloured fur and trims on skirts and dresses, and panels on coats. Bolero jackets and shawls added a touch of glamour to a collection of rich tones of purple, emerald green and royal blue on girls wearing barely-there make-up and pulled-back hair.

But perhaps the most impressive presentation of all was a version of the Spring/Summer 2008 collection (which had been shown three weeks previously in Milan) staged at a truly extraordinary location: the Great Wall of China. This ambitious and extravagant event (it is said to have cost $10 million) was unprecedented, and further consolidated Fendi's place internationally. The 500 exclusive guests sat on seated seats (Kate Bosworth, Thandiwe Newton and Julia

ABOVE A stunning Fendi presentation at the Great Wall of China, where 88 models paraded along a catwalk that was 88 metres (290 feet) long.

OVERLEAF Spring/Summer 2013 was a graphic collection using traditional methods. In the designer's own words, a case of "doing modern our way, with our techniques".

Restoin Roitfeld were among the front row VIPs), were given complimentary Fendi handwarmers and served hot chocolate after the presentation. The show began with 88 models (a number symbolizing good luck in Chinese culture) walking gracefully in procession down the "catwalk" as the sun set. On either side of them rose imposing mountains on which double F logos were projected. The models wore long, full, delicate skirts with irresistible textures that ended above the ankle, and classic belted dresses in red – also symbolizing Chinese good fortune – and black, hinting at a 1950s aesthetic. There were also white mini structured dresses and tailored trouser suits, in delicate

OPPOSITE
Celebrating their
90-year anniversary,
Fendi chose Rome's
iconic Fontana di
Trevi to present their
latest collection on
7 July 2016.

BELOW A patterned
grey pouch with a
golden handle is the
perfect accessory
for a show whose
official hashtag
was #Legendsand-
Fairytales

mesh and woven leather, with a colour scheme that included a great deal of beige, splashes of yellow, green, pink and blue, as well as some bold patterns on silk and satin, including a pattern of recurring circles. The looks were accessorized with high heels, handbags and some perfectly fitted, cropped, fur bolero jackets. The once small family business was now very much on the world stage, and everyone was watching.

Fendi's first Haute Fourrure (Haute Fur) show, Autumn/Winter 2015, marked the 50-year partnership with Lagerfeld as their Creative Director. Titled Silver Moon, it was shown as part of the Paris schedule and, as anticipated, was a spectacle for the eyes. It showcased fur panels, appliqué and filigree embroidery embellishments, as well as new techniques such as fur sealed with silver, recreating a stunning metallic effect. A black mink coat with a feathered collar, which had taken

PREVIOUS The couture finale, showing the models standing on the fountain's pool covered by a sheet of glass, making them look like they were walking on water, 2016.

RIGHT Lagerfeld and Venturini Fendi graciously acknowledging the audience at the end of their legendary 2016 show.

20 people 200 hours to make, was another example of Fendi's outstanding abilities.

To celebrate its 90th anniversary, another Fendi dream was realized for the second Haute Fourrure show in Autumn/ Winter 2016 couture, which Lagerfeld himself described as "magical". This time, their spellbinding show took place at the iconic Trevi Fountain, a truly fitting venue given the brand's strong Roman roots. It had recently been given a facelift, with Fendi contributing some €2.6 million towards its restoration, in a project that had taken four years from conception to completion. Guests were flown in by private jet from the Paris collections to enjoy a presentation aptly called Legends and Fairy Tales. The show was a turning point for the house, opened by model Kendall Jenner wearing a fitted navy buttoned dress, and the collection showcased unique hand-painted items, intricate embroidery on garments and fur intarsia. Adding to the illusion, marble and stones were printed on soft surfaces like mink, silk and organza – as Venturini Fendi explained to *CNN Style*: "I like something that looks hard, (but) when you touch it it's soft." The girls walked onto a clear plexiglass catwalk, as if gliding on the water itself, and looked like Pre-Raphaelite muses. They wore florals, perhaps inspired by Northern European prints, chiffon and delicate A-line gowns worn with short-laced boots, in a timeless show that was traditional and contemporary in equal measure. Model Bella Hadid closed the spectacle wearing a stunning fur cape and, as is customary, Lagerfeld and Venturini Fendi came out at the end to take a bow. As they walked side by side to face the audience, Karl nonchalantly threw a coin into the fountain.

Also as part of the 90th anniversary, an exhibition called *FENDI ROMA – The Artisans of Dreams* explored the house's sublime work at their headquarters, Palazzo della Civiltà Italiana, in a show that celebrated the history and tradition of their craftsmen and women.

Spring/Summer 2017 highlighted plenty of Fendi's personality in a show – based on Marie Antoinette – that was simultaneously feminine and bold. On display were oversized sunglasses, striped aprons tied with ribbons (creating a cascading effect), culotte trousers and short sock-boots. These were matched with plunging geometrical necklines on

LEFT Kendall Jenner wears a Fendi monogrammed bag and matching printed Fendi fur bomber jacket in the Spring/Summer 2018 show.

OPPOSITE Triangular shoulders and cinched waistlines featured heavily in the Spring/Summer 2018 collection.

resses and tops with balloon sleeves. Delicate, structured puffball shapes, sheer silk garments, cut-out fabric, embroidery and opulent brocades added to this eclectic look, which was primarily in pastel colours, accentuated with neon accessories. In his notes Lagerfeld described the collection as inspired by a "modern rococo muse" and explained, "It takes the best elements from the past but then creates something from our day."

Fendi's Haute Couture show for Autumn/Winter 2018 was another dreamy collection that began with bright primary colours and tailed off to a muted palette of nudes, white, lilacs, as well as black looks, finishing with soft pink glamorous looks that had a classic Hollywood elegance to them. Embellished with feathers and delicate embroidery, it featured defined yet feminine silhouettes – some sheer and some textured. Interestingly, the house included fur alternatives for this show and treated them to look like fur, something Lagerfeld had always wanted to do – frayed chiffon made to look like mink and sequins resembling astrakhan. While the brand has faced ongoing criticism from anti-fur organizations and many luxury houses are becoming fur-free, Fendi maintains that everyone is free to make their choices and that it's a natural material. "It's part of our history," says Silvia Venturini Fendi.

For Spring/Summer 2019 the house presented a sensual collection in earthy tones that was glamorous and intellectually upbeat. And while it didn't have an official name, Lagerfeld liked calling it GP (giant pockets), which also stands for Grand Prix – as Silvia Venturini Fendi pointed out. From an opening on the wall shaped like a red circle with a sideways golden F on it, the girls emerged, one by one, onto a long catwalk in a pink room. Pockets, usually discreetly tucked to the sides or inside the garments, were oversized, and the focus of many looks.

OPPOSITE
Autumn/Winter
2019 was the last
collection that Karl
Lagerfeld designed
for the house.
Strong collars and
tailoring defined
the show.

Cycling shorts and utilitarian belts (to carry a phone and other tech) were featured, as were adaptations of the Fendi Baguette and the Peekaboo in a nod to a sports aesthetic.

The Autumn/Winter 2019 presentation was emotional as it was to be the last collection Lagerfeld designed for Fendi: he died just three days before the show he had hoped to attend. It was a beautiful, feminine and very chic collection that encapsulated the breadth of his wisdom: leather was perforated to have a fishnet finish and sheer layers were superimposed on each other, creating a beautiful flow. A-line shapes, wasp waists and sharp shoulders featured on dresses and flowing skirts (some pleated), while Edwardian bows on the neck and angular collars reminded the audience of the designer himself. A colour palette of mostly earthy tones was set back with the occasional garment in bright yellow, pink or turquoise blue, and with red accessories. There were mink garments and sheer tights, as well as tops with a pattern called *Karligraphy* (the version of the double F logo created in his own handwriting in 1981), which was also on the clasp of some of the leather handbags. The soundtrack for this show was curated by Michel Gaubert and Ryan Aguilar, in a fitting mixtape that included David Bowie's inspiring song "Heroes". Silvia, alone, appeared at the end to take a bow and to acknowledge the audience.

Karl Lagerfeld's death in February 2019 reverberated throughout the fashion industry. Fendi had lost not only a designer and its creative driving force but an honorary family member too. It was now time for Silvia Venturini Fendi to begin her own story, always honouring and remembering her mentor and predecessor Karl. Speaking to *CNN Style*, she said: "Of course, today we have to turn the page, but, and this is probably something very Roman, to write the future you have to be able to read the past."

BELOW The Palatine Hill in Rome was the chosen location for a collection dedicated to Karl Lagerfeld, showcasing 54 looks, reflecting the number of years he worked for Fendi.

OVERLEAF Fendi Men's Spring/Summer 2017 was a light-hearted collection complete with a swimming pool and a diving board in *Fendi* yellow.

"Nothing is impossible"
– Fendi family motto

Forever classic despite its constant reinvention, Fendi Menswear remains a pioneer in innovative concepts, ideas and hi-tech challenges. Introduced in 1990, as an extension of the brand's portfolio of offerings, it once again demonstrated Fendi's unique experimental approach to fashion and love of contrasts. Since its inception it has been recognized for its classic elegant lines and sensuous textures, as well as for its brilliant intellectual approach and elaborate processes. Silvia, who has been heading this department since 1992, loves to play with reality and to tell a story, and despite the brand's commitment to excellence and almost obsessive attention to detail, a sense of humour – and sometimes a touch of irony – is never too far away.

The Sun and Fun-themed Spring/Summer 2017 show, for example, recreating a Mediterranean villa on the runway, was inspired by artists' summer ensembles, including what Dalí, Hockney and Picasso wore when on holiday. The catwalk featured a long stretch of pool, complete with a yellow branded diving board poised at one end, which was in turn surrounded by perfectly manicured grass. Models walked out through French doors with wooden shutters and down the edge of the pool wearing the iconic Fendi Pequin Stripe in a number of vibrant expressions, classic terry towelling garments and robes. Slip-on shoes and playful bags – some heavily branded, others decorated with free-style, multi-coloured abstract faces – completed the look: true Italian poolside chic.

For the Spring/Summer 2019 menswear show, Fendi collaborated with Italian artist Nico Vascellari, Delfina Delettrez's partner, who reworked Fendi's legendary logo (for

OPPOSITE A terry towelling short-sleeved jacket is accessorized with a striped bag and poolside sliders in the Spring/Summer 2017 show.

LEFT Spring/
Summer 2018 was a
show that combined
formalwear with
shorts, a style Silvia
Venturini Fendi
referred to as the
"Skype Look", formal
above the waist and
casual below.

OPPOSITE A
small briefcase
with delicate
illustrations is the
perfect companion
to a classic tailored
checked suit.

one season only!). The show's mood was dark and the clothes were light (there were some almost see-through bomber jackets) in a casual collection of clean lines using a '70s colour palette – with many logos, check patterns and a mixture of formal and casual attire.

For Autumn/Winter 2019, Venturini Fendi found inspiration in Karl Lagerfeld's very own style, and explored this by contrasting it with athleisure, bringing them both together. For this show Fendi collaborated with Tokyo-based company Porter-Yoshida & Co., known for their engineered work with nylon, to adapt some of the men's bags, including the first Fendi Baguette and Peekaboo for men (complete with thick straps that can be tied at the waist). This functional fabric was used, as well as other finishes, such as shearling, prints, metallic leather and plenty of personality.

Spring/Summer 2020 had a great cinematic feel, as this season's collaborator was Oscar-winning film director Luca Guadagnino, with music written by Japanese composer Ryuichi Sakamoto. The evocative show was set in Milan's bucolic Villa Reale gardens and explored the duality between the simplicity and the complexity of nature – nature, as described by Silvia herself, being the greatest act of creativity. Based on prints sketched by Guadagnino, the looks had a practical and utilitarian feel: shirts, tops, jumpers, trousers and suits as well as some capes (reminiscent of the film-maker's Ethiopian connection as a child) came in earthy colours, and there was even a denim jumpsuit, accessorized with a thin belt and sandals. As always, lots of accessories: sunglasses, floaty hats, bags, baskets and crossbodies, and gardening references, such as watering cans and gloves, completed this elegant and romantic modern-outdoor look. The shoes were a collaboration between the house and Japanese shoemakers MoonStar, founded in 1873 and known for their traditional rubber-crafting techniques.

In contrast, transformation and adaptability, in its many forms, was the theme for the Autumn/Winter 2020 show. Our perception of classic tailoring was challenged: clever looks included panelled coats (in fur or flannel) that could be worn long length, as a standard jacket or even as a short bolero by unzipping the relevant sections, and there were branded yellow bags in different sizes, which looked like paper carrier bags but were, in fact, made of leather. More Fendi yellow was on Baguettes, scarves, suits and outerwear, and chunky boots, trainers and hi-tops, which accessorized the outfits. To finish, the four looks that had been created in collaboration with Kunihiko Morinaga from Tokyo-based Anrealage were placed

OPPOSITE Spring/ Summer 2020 was a presentation inspired by nature. Here, a model wears a textured leather coat over an olive-green shirt and ochre culottes.

RIGHT Silvia Venturini Fendi's love of nature and adventure was apparent in her Spring/Summer 2020 collection, which included explorer-inspired looks.

OPPOSITE Silvia Venturini Fendi said her starting point for the Menswear Autumn/Winter 2020 was "to work on the essentials of the classic wardrobe of a man of tomorrow".

RIGHT A model wears a knitted cardigan, bag and a branded oversized Fendi scarf in its legendary yellow hue for Autumn/Winter 2020.

OPPOSITE Autumn/Winter 2020 included a classic suit in two-tone yellow, accessorized with chunky branded boots and a small leather bag in chocolate brown.

OVERLEAF A mac lined with the double F logo designed by Lagerfeld in 1965 and maroon leather trousers for Autumn/Winter 2022.

under UV lights. While the uptempo music was playing, the light-sensitive photochromic materials on the coats, hats, gloves and bags were activated and slowly changed colour (some from white to yellow, others to reveal a pattern), an effect that would also take place when in contact with sunshine. The message? Things are not always what they seem…

Entitled "What is Normal Today", Autumn/Winter 2021 was a colourful collection that included shades of bright ochre, bottle green, electric blue and fuchsia. It displayed interesting modern shapes: three-quarter length trouser suits, belted short jackets, long gabardines, loose-fitting trousers and padded garments. The industrial-looking catwalk was digitally masterminded by Nico Vascellari, who constructed this immersive experience with neon tubes, creating a geometric installation, and an upbeat techno soundtrack that included Silvia's voiceover as if she was talking on the phone.

The elegance and quality synonymous with Fendi were present in Autumn/Winter 2022, a show of clean lines, which merged quirky androgynous – sometimes deconstructed – silhouettes: long trousers that were skirts from the back, oversized gabardine coats, short boxy bolero jackets with three-quarter length sleeves and a tux, à la James Bond, complete with a striking bow tie. Loafers, trainers, bucket hats and logo print bags were among the accessories completing the look as they made their way confidently down a metallic platform shaped like a double F that ended in a ramp. Spring/Summer 2023 offered plenty of skate-park-style denim and frayed edges, even on accessories such as bags – evoking luxe sport. The collection merged tailoring, sometimes deconstructed, with leather jackets and blazers to be enjoyed in the sunshine. Chunky pool sliders, trainers and loafers defined the accessories, which included some of Delfina Delettrez's finest jewellery designs.

OPPOSITE Trainers and understated jewellery dress down this tailored ensemble complete with a bucket hat and a Baguette handbag for Autumn/Winter 2022.

LEFT Model wears a blue knitted top with a fringed visor hat.

OPPOSITE A branded Fendi bucket hat in fringed denim with matching shorts gave this collection a summery feel in the Spring/Summer 2023 show.

THE WORLD'S
FIRST "IT" BAG

THE BAGUETTE

"The Baguette is like a best friend that never leaves your side" – Silvia Venturini Fendi

In 1997, Silvia Venturini Fendi designed the now-legendary Baguette handbag. "I was asked to come up with a particularly easy and functional handbag," she told *Glass* magazine. "It had to be technological and minimal, just like the times. My response was the 'Baguette' – the exact opposite of what was requested of me." The bag, which sits comfortably under your arm, like a loaf of French bread, is very simple and has plenty of Parisian flair, as does a smaller chic version, often referred to as its sister style – the Croissant. With its short strap, compact rectangular shape, unmistakable "double F" logo clasp, a flap, and the ability to be dressed up or down, the Baguette has become so iconic that over a million people own one today, with fresh chameleonic iterations being introduced seasonally, enticing new and existing customers.

OPPOSITE A satin Fendi Baguette embellished with beads and crystals.

Baguettes first appeared on the catwalk in Fendi's
Autumn/Winter 1997 show, bursting with attitude – some
were embroidered, some featured sequins, some were plain,
and some striped, but they all had plenty of character. The
overwhelming impact of the Baguette took Fendi by surprise
– as Venturini Fendi remarked, "It was the start of a new
movement. It signalled the end of minimalism and the start
of a new era." These handbags were sublime: handcrafted
in Italy and using premium leather and other exquisite
materials, which resulted in a very hefty price tag. Such was
their success, they were later credited with coining the term
"It" bag.

When the Baguette launched, Fendi had only five stores
and was very much a family-run business (today, they have
over 200). But as soon as Madonna purchased one, its success
was unprecedented. Without the production infrastructure

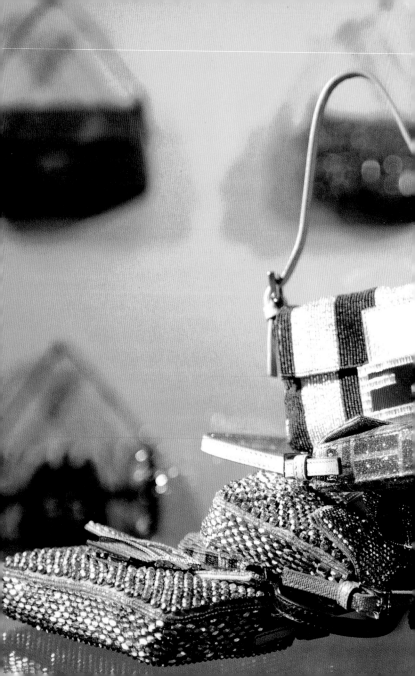

in place, Fendi struggled to produce the bag in the numbers wanted, and the difficulty of obtaining one outside Italy caused plenty of elbowing in-store. This only added to its cult status and long waiting lists were created for fashionistas worldwide. The Baguette became so popular that it was seen everywhere, and despite its unmistakable shape, took many different guises.

But its mass appeal came through HBO's comedy drama *Sex and the City* (1998–2004), whose stylish protagonist Carrie Bradshaw (played by Sarah Jessica Parker) was rarely seen without one. The Baguette even starred in episode 17 in the third series (aired in 2000), when Bradshaw takes a wrong turn in downtown New York, somewhere south of Houston Street, and is mugged at gunpoint. When asked to hand over her precious purple sequinned bag, she is both crestfallen and shocked by the aggressor's fashion ignorance, bravely correcting him before reluctantly handing it over: "It's a Baguette," she explains. The bag, now a legendary status symbol, has been seen over the years on the crook of the arm of endless celebrities, including Naomi Campbell, Julia Roberts, Gwyneth Paltrow, Paris Hilton, Mary J. Blige and Jennifer Lopez, as well as Sophia Loren, who once remarked that the Baguette was like a drug, and who is, according to *Vogue*, a proud owner of at least 10. More recently, it's been spotted under the arms of Kate Moss, Lily Allen, Kim Kardashian and Gigi Hadid, to name but a few.

The Baguette bag reached its peak in the 2000s with the logomania boom but was eventually discontinued. Then, in 2012, 15 years after it was designed, a coffee table book called *Fendi Baguette* was published. With 250 extraordinary images of the bag in its many different forms – from acid tones to fur trims, sheared mink, beads and tassels patterns, exotic skins and denim – it captures the spirit of the coveted Fendi Baguette, which has been produced in over 1,000 models and

collected the world over. Celebrating the artistry behind the Baguette, the book displays the broad range of its designs as well as some Baguettes from limited edition collaborations with artists including Damien Hirst and Jeff Koons, all of which perfectly lend themselves to be worn with confidence, tucked under one's arm. Six Baguette styles were reissued to celebrate the milestone.

A fun digital campaign called #BaguetteFriendsForever celebrated the iconic bag in 2019, in a series of short films that celebrate friendship. The casting was a mix of actresses, models, DJs, dancers and influencers, with storylines centred around the Baguette. One of the films, shot in New York, follows a group of girlfriends, one of whom has her heart set on a purple sequinned Baguette she's seen online. When they arrive at the endi store, the shop assistant tells them that someone has just bought the last one, so they run after the lucky shopper shouting, "Wait! I need that bag!" The customer in question happens to be Sarah Jessica Parker, who turns around elegantly on her heels, bag in arm, and replies: "This isn't a bag, it's a Baguette." New versions of the bag were now available; a larger one has detachable straps so the bag can be worn crossbody, but, as Silvia told *Harper's Bazaar Australia*, "they all embody the Fendi DNA." Another TV appearance that reinforced its celebrated status took place in January 2022, in episode 9 "No Strings Attached" of *SATC*'s sequel, *And Just Like That…* This time it was a magenta sequin Baguette, a collaboration between SJP and Fendi, which was later available online.

In 2020, Silvia Venturini Fendi headed a project called Hand in Hand aimed to encourage, support and preserve the rich tapestry of Italian artisanship. Through this project, as she explains, the brand invited 20 workshops, one from each Italian region, and worked with people who have been cultivating techniques and skills through generations – some of them for centuries – to create their very own interpretations of the bag. The initiative is, therefore, a celebration of the craftsmen and women who, behind the scenes, made these limited edition Baguettes: in Venturini Fendi's words, "showing what's behind a beautiful product". In turn, the project supported the artisans, whom she refers to as artists, helping to preserve these old-time techniques. The inside pocket of every Hand in Hand bag is stamped with the workshop's denomination of origin, as well as the project's trademark.

The first example of this was a Baguette that debuted in the Autumn/Winter 2020 show: made in Tuscany (in the Florentine atelier Peroni) from a single piece of leather, it was hand-moulded with no stitching. Another example is the wicker bag from Italy's Marche region, specifically from

OVERLEAF A blue and pink sequin Fendi Baguette shown during London Fashion Week, 2023.

the Bottega Intreccio workshop, where willow branches were carefully woven with techniques used since the Renaissance. There was also a striking version decorated with an embroidery technique called *bandera*, with raised floral motifs. For the Fendi project, Consolata Pralormo Design (from the Piedmont region) used traditional pink, Savoy blue and green in a manufacturing process that is particularly close to Silvia's heart, as she remembers two armchairs in her great-grandmother Paola's living room with *bandera* embroidery. It takes approximately 50 hours to execute this embroidery style for a single Fendi Baguette. Marking the bag's 25th anniversary, Fendi published a book, also called *Hand in Hand*, celebrating these true masterpieces, and – of course – the custodians who hand down the precious techniques through generations.

As part of the celebrations for the Baguette's 25th anniversary in 2022, the icon was reimagined in unprecedented ways. Kim Jones, Fendi's Artistic Director of Womenswear, didn't want to present a traditional collection to mark the

RIGHT Kim Jones (left) and Marc Jacobs collaborated for the Fendi Spring 2023 fashion show at the Hammerstein Ballroom in September 2022, in New York City.

occasion. "It's a celebration of a time," he told *Vogue*, "of
the moment the Baguette became famous. I relate that time
to a sense of freedom in excess and fun – both qualities the
Baguette possesses."

An accessories campaign was shot by Steven Meisel, fittingly
fronted by supermodel Linda Evangelista, a pivotal moment that
marked her modelling comeback. She posted one of the images
on her personal Instagram account (beautifully accessorized
with dusty pink gloves, pink sunglasses, earrings, several silver
Baguettes in different sizes and three baseball caps worn one on
top of the other), announcing Fendi's upcoming show:

"On September 9 2022 @Fendi will host a special fashion

show in New York City to celebrate the 25th anniversary of the #FendiBaguette, designed by @silviaventurinifendi, and two years since @mrkimjones joined the Maison as Artistic Director of Couture and Womenswear. #Fendi."

And special it was. Fendi's Resort 2023 collection was a party to remember and an ode to the original "It" bag, presented at Manhattan's Hammerstein Ballroom in New York, the city that made it legendary. To open the show, Kim Jones came onto the stage and pulled down the curtain to reveal a floor-to-ceiling mirror, adding a touch of drama. Grace Jones was in the audience, as were Kate Moss, Amber Valletta, Christy Turlington and Kim Kardashian. Then the lights went up and Lila Grace Moss Hack was the first to walk down the catwalk. The collection was very late '90s New York, in a nod to the TV show that helped its launch to stratospheric fame, and was a mix of styles: there was mohair, chiffon, silk, a muted palette with accents of neon shades, plenty of layering and gaiters – reminiscent of legwarmers. And the Baguette itself, the real hero and a fashion institution, came in endless and unimaginable shapes and sizes, carried in pairs or more, some embellished with silver beads, some with Swarovski crystals, there was even a shopper that had a holder in which to place your classic Baguette. It was all about the Baguette – some of the collection's looks featuring up to 20 of them (including charm-sized bags and nano Baguettes incorporated into hats, gloves, even socks and legwarmers). And when asked during the fittings how many bags would appear on the runway, Venturini Fendi said it was impossible to count them all.

The show was divided into three sections. First there was a timeless classic Fendi story with short skirts, sequins, layers and fitted dresses. Then followed the Tiffany & Co. collaboration, featuring Baguettes with diamonds, available in Tiffany blue – silk, satin or leather – with sterling silver or gold-plated

OPPOSITE Bella Hadid walks the Fendi catwalk in a "Tiffany blue" jumpsuit and a bag necklace, as part of the Tiffany & Co. collaboration.

OVERLEAF Two mini Fendi Baguettes as worn by a fashionista during Autumn/Winter Milan Fashion Week, 2020.

hardware and detachable straps; and in three sizes – medium, nano and pico, the charm size, encapsulating the timeless elegance of *Breakfast at Tiffany's*. The final fashion story was the Marc Jacobs collaboration, which he called FENDIROMA "because it sounded like an amusement park or something fun." Jacobs stamped his unmistakable font to the legendary bag, creating his urban "downtown NY" version, which included some denim, crop tops, fun oversized repurposed fur hats, utilitarian silhouettes, terry towelling jacquard and plenty of branding.

Other collaborations included Japanese brand Porter, specialists in nylon, thus embracing an athleisure aesthetic (also seen at the menswear Autumn/Winter 22 show) and Sarah Jessica Parker, who designed a capsule collection in degradé

OPPOSITE A beanie hat with a turn-up brim is decorated with a mini Baguette featuring a matching-colour Fendi buckle.

BELOW Delfina Delettrez, Silvia Venturini Fendi, Linda Evangelista, Marc Jacobs and Kim Jones go onstage to close the 25th anniversary celebration of the Baguette.

sequins in wasabi green, baby pink, turquoise blue and purple (the purple colour was available only in London's New Bond Street store, Rome's Palazzo Fendi boutique and the New York boutique on 57th Street). When the show ended, the huge mirror at the back of the stage became a glass wall, revealing the models standing behind it, as if in a shop window. Then, Kim Jones, Silvia Venturini-Fendi, Delfina Delettrez, Marc Jacobs and Linda Evangelista (marking her fashion comeback) came to take a bow. Evangelista was wearing a Tiffany blue opera cape and held a unique Baguette masterpiece in sterling silver: part of the Hand in Hand initiative, and the first in the project to be made outside of Italy, this was a collaboration between Fendi and Tiffany & Co. The piece is engraved with lilies, Italy's national flower, and roses, emblematic of New York State. Using a traditional chasing technique to decorate the piece, this Baguette took approximately 250 hours to make, over a period of four months.

OPPOSITE Sarah Jessica Parker holds a sequinned purple Baguette on the set of *And Just Like That...*, the sequel to *Sex and the City*, at Webster Hall, New York City, 2021.

BELOW Many Baguettes, in different sizes, fabrics and textures were brought together to celebrate the 25th anniversary of Silvia Venturini Fendi's iconic design.

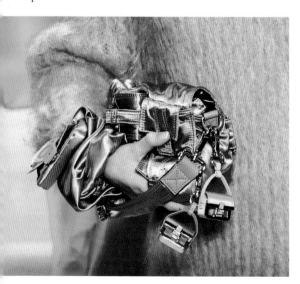

A NEW ERA
FOR FENDI

TAKING FENDI
FORWARD

"The thing I want to do, looking at the archive of Fendi and then looking at it now, is to really lighten it" – Kim Jones in conversation with *Harper's Bazaar*

Fendi's Spring/Summer 2021 couture show was the start of a new chapter for the legendary fashion house. It marked British designer Kim Jones's debut as their womenswear artistic director, making him only the second designer to work for the once family-run business. Jones, whose role is to oversee ready-to-wear, haute couture and fur for women, replaced Karl Lagerfeld – Silvia Venturini Fendi had held that position in the transitional period between 2019 and 2020. Not only was this Jones's first collection for the House, it was also his first ever couture show. In a warm message welcoming him to the "Fendi family", Silvia announced that she was "looking forward to tak[ing] the Fendi universe to the next level with him" to which he replied that it was a "true honour as a designer to be able to join the house of Fendi".

OPPOSITE Kate Moss wears a stunning silver gown designed by Kim Jones for his first Fendi collection, Spring/Summer 2021, during the Paris Haute Couture Fashion Week.

BELOW Actress
Demi Moore walks
the catwalk for
Spring/Summer
2021, the brand's
first Spring/
Summer haute
couture show.

Jones's work has brought a fresh, modern perspective to the house and – as Lagerfeld did with the Fendi sisters – he collaborates closely with the current generations of Fendi women – Silvia Venturini Fendi and her daughters, Delfina and Leonetta – as well as with creative consultant Amanda Harlech (who worked closely with Karl Lagerfeld for over 20 years) and his design director and right-hand person Lucy Beeden, with whom he first teamed up with for his St Martins graduation show. Through them, and thanks to his extensive research into the precious Fendi archives, he arrives at plenty of ideas which translate into constant reinterpretations of the essence of the Fendi DNA, embodied in its matriarchs. As explained by Delfina: "I always say that my mother is the Fendi archive and I am the walking archive."

Jones began designing for Fendi in lockdown and was restricted to research from within the confines of his London home. "I had to look at what I had in my house," he said. Being an avid rare book collector, he found inspiration in Virginia Woolf's book, *Orlando: A Biography* (1928), of which he owns nine copies (including the one Woolf presented to Vita Sackville-West). The novel, inspired by the author's lover, Vita Sackville-West, describes the life of a poet who lives for centuries and changes from male to female, themes that resonated creatively with the designer. More widely, he referenced the Bloomsbury Set, a group of intellectuals and artists that included Woolf, and also Charleston, which became the group's rural retreat. After some delving, he connected these figures of the early twentieth century to Fendi's Roman heritage through the artist Vanessa Bell (who was Virginia

ABOVE Unusually, some menswear was present in Kim Jones's debut collection. Here, a model wears black tailoring.

OVERLEAF Naomi Campbell wears an imposing cape as part of the collection inspired by Virginia Woolf's novel, *Orlando*.

Woolf's sister). She lived at Charleston with the artist Duncan Grant, and produced a series of paintings of the gardens of Rome's Villa Borghese. It became the starting point for this magical collection, which he called the "journey from Bloomsbury to Borghese". "I thought there was a really nice story between the strong women – the Fendis – and celebrating the Bloomsbury Group," said Jones.

This, his first show for the house, was revealed during Milan Fashion Week in February 2021 and marked a new direction, being the first ever Spring/Summer couture collection for Fendi, which took the focus away from fur. And while fully respecting the Fendi code, the live-streamed presentation was the designer's very own personal take on couture, underpinned by showcasing the extensive skills of the brand's artisans. Here, Kim Jones surrounded himself with his very own set, which included some younger members of their families as well as friends, such as actress Demi Moore, model Kate Moss (who was appointed his accessories consultant "because," he told *Harper's Bazaar*, "she has got the best taste in the world") and her daughter, Lila Grace Moss Hack, Christy Turlington and her nephew, James Turlington, Adwoa Aboah and her sister, Kesewa Aboah, as well as Silvia Venturini Fendi's own daughters, Leonetta Fendi and Delfina Delettrez. "I wanted to recruit all the women I admire and trust around me," he said. Silvia collaborated by creating accessories for the collection: she used Lagerfeld's archive calligraphy on shoes and mother of pearl minaudières to inscribe lines from *Orlando*. Delfina Delettrez provided the jewellery, which included beautiful beaded black headdresses and some precious Murano glass droplets that followed the shape of the ear. The legendary Sam McKnight was in charge of the hair (he created a fresh "caught out in the rain" wet look, suggestive of an elegant Renaissance style) and Peter Philips did the make-up, playing on gender

fluidity and gender-blurring: his women's make-up was
understated, but he used strong defined red lips on the men.

The performance was beautiful, theatrical and romantic,
with a timeless quality and rich references, telling a story
through its intricate clothes and bringing literature and fashion
together. Models from across the generations, some holding
metal-bound book clutches, walked down a glass labyrinth
installation (shaped like the interlocking double F logo, from a
bird's-eye view) and was lined with trees and priceless antique
books on shelves, curated by Peter Harrington Rare Books.
Contemporary composer Max Richter created the score for
the show, which had a voice-over containing extracts from the

correspondence between Woolf and Sackville-West, beautifully read by Fendi friends (Isabella Rossellini, Christina Ricci, Moss and Aboah) and family members. After walking down a central catwalk, the models took their positions in enclosed glass cubicles, where they stood still, as if daydreaming and watching the world go by. They wore long regal-looking capes in silver (made with incredible textures, some with marble effects), silk dresses and dark trouser suits for men with a 1920s feel to them (this was significant because there are no menswear couture collections as such). The show also displayed intarsia skins, hand-embroidered flowers in blush pink, garments painted by hand and delicate jewellery, all of which came together to create a timeless fantasy.

A book called *The Fendi Set* was published in 2022 to accompany the collection. A tribute to the Bloomsbury Set, it also explored Fendi's connection to them. Photographed by Nikolai von Bismarck, who combined different media, including Polaroids and Super 8 stills, the book is a collage of letters and notes from members of the early twentieth-century set. Models, including Christy Turlington, Demi Moore, Cara Delevingne, Kate Moss and Lila Grace Moss Hack, Bella Hadid and Naomi Campbell, were shot in a number of locations where the Bloomsbury Set had once gathered – Charleston, Knole, Sissinghurst Castle – as well as in Rome's Villa Medici and Villa Borghese buildings. The textured images, which are sometimes blurred, have a rich quality to them, reminiscent of a Victorian photo album. "I wanted a ghostly atmosphere, a dreamlike quality," Kim Jones told *AnOther Magazine*. "*Orlando* is about time travelling and I wanted the work to transcend time, to drift between the present, past and future."

In contrast, the British designer's Autumn/Winter 2021 show was an extremely Italian collection, evoking the very

OPPOSITE An eye-catching "tricolore" marabou jacket is worn with a pair of rose gold silk trousers.

OPPOSITE A
stunning floor-
length dress
inspired by archive
illustrations from
Antonio Lopez.

essence of the Fendi brand under the stylish Fendi sisters. This time, Roman-looking ruins, placed in glass enclosures reminiscent of a museum, acted as the backdrop to the show. It displayed classic elegance with a modern twist: there were belted coats, high boots, shirts, sensual dresses and fringing on garments in a palette of quintessentially Fendi earthy and neutral tones – including camel, blush, taupe – as well as black and white. The final black tailored looks were said to be a nod to Delfina Delettrez, who was wearing a black tuxedo when she first met Kim Jones. There was also an interesting statement piece: an upcycled long-haired fox coat that had been made from the remnants of previous pieces. Not only was this a welcome challenge for the Fendi artisans, but perhaps also a glimpse into the future of Fendi Furs. A Hand in Hand Baguette made in the region of Campania also appeared in this show. This superb masterpiece was made by the Stinga Tarsia workshop, using local briar root and maple wood, with delicate inlays throughout, using a local technique called *tarsia lignea sorrentina*.

Spring/Summer 2022 was Jones's first live show for Fendi. It was another elegant performance bursting with Italian flavour, this time with a strong Studio 54/1970s influence, inspired by archive material from the visionary fashion illustrator Antonio Lopez – a close friend of Karl Lagerfeld's. It presented tailoring that came in at the waist with narrow logoed belts, dresses with lots of fringing and some full-length gowns with beautiful diagonal stripes in pale pink, gold, white, fuchsia and purple, and matching bags. The fabric on these dresses also featured a Fendi sub-pattern (from an archived logo sketched by Lopez), adding a hint of disco glamour to the already luxe look. Accessories included plexiglass jewellery in the shape of lily leaves with gold detailing (inspired by Lopez), and high boots. The compelling colours of this collection were built up

gradually – starting with white, grey and shades of brown that moved to some lilac, fuchsia and pastel-coloured garments. It ended with shades of brown and black.

The starting point for Jones's Autumn/Winter 2022 collection was a 1986 Fendi blouse that Delfina was wearing one day in the Rome office. Designed by Lagerfeld, and inspired by the Memphis Group aesthetic, it had once belonged to her mother. "I took it off her back and put it on the research rail," said Jones. The collection was very 1980s in its feel – strong shoulders and power-dressing shirts – but also took inspiration from Fendi's Spring/Summer 2000 show (a feminine collection that utilized light and flowing fabrics). The result was a very modern and relevant look with some considered tailoring that used fabrics mostly associated with menswear. This lightness continued in his Autumn/Winter 2022 couture show, which was delicate and elegant in equal measure. Presented in a completely brilliant white room, it included some exquisite pieces – classic tan leather looks, Japanese kimonos that had been woven in Kyoto, and some sparkling see-through ethereal dresses worthy of a red-carpet event. Muted colours were intercepted by neon yellow, mint and navy-blue dresses.

Jones's retrospective approach proceeded to bring past collections into the present. For his next show he looked at Karl Lagerfeld's work between 1996 and 2000. "It's about continuity," he said. "I am interested in looking at things that Karl has done, and seeing how we can develop them – both visually and technically." Spring/Summer 2023 reflected this spirit in a ready-to-wear collection that was full of contrasts: natural shades – so associated with the brand – with pops of summery colours (watermelon red, apple green and cornflower blue), shiny silk skirts worn with textured knitted jumpers or athleisure paired with traditional timeless shapes. There were

OPPOSITE Spring/ Summer 2022 was a collection with a strong 1970s influence. Thigh-high boots complete this pastel look.

classic pieces, such as fitted single-breasted overcoats with stand
collars and an obi belt knotted at the back, and some strong
accessories: rounded-toe platform boots made of patent leather
with an FF embossed sole, and platform slides made of blue
mink or Nappa leather (which came in white, green, pink and
beige). Bags came in different sizes, and included a leather bag
inspired by a paper shopping bag (echoing a 1994 collection)
and a micro version worn as a pendant.

RIGHT Pink mink
sliders add a touch
of glamour to this
casual look.

OPPOSITE Fendi's
Spring/Summer
2023 presentation
was mostly in
neutral colours,
with some outfits
in beautiful
pistachio green and
watermelon pink.

With this in mind, Jones stated that his Spring/Summer 2023 couture presentation was "a continuation" of his Autumn/Winter couture show, in response to a high demand for evening gowns. The collection galvanized the new Fendi aesthetic: 39 impeccable dresses, mostly full-length in delicate colours, that draped and looked like ancient Roman marble statues – just as Lagerfeld had once achieved. Jones's use of leather, which looked and felt like fabric (some garments even had printed lace patterns on them), showcased Fendi's heritage: "I wanted to really work with the couture techniques, what they can do now is so advanced."

Duality, such an integral theme to Fendi, was key in the Autumn/Winter 2023 show. It also explored androgyny in a collection that combined men's tailoring and classic femininity, recalibrating our perception of Fendi. Inspired by Delfina Delettrez ("It all started with Delfina," said Jones), the collection featured bias-cut trousers, double-collared jackets, macs that revealed sequins in their lining, and suits combined with pleated skirts in brown and in shades of blue – the colours of Delfina's Roman school uniform. The models walked to upbeat electronic music, through what appeared to be a tunnel of light that originated from a brightly-lit wall behind their starting point. Shapes were deconstructed and restructured in asymmetrical ways, referencing punk styling and defying expectations. The last looks to walk the catwalk, in magenta and orange, were said to be inspired by a Lagerfeld sketch from 1996. Thigh-high lace-up boots and jewellery with the double F logo were among the key accessories, which also included the latest handbag: the Fendi Multi. This can be worn as two distinct silhouettes in a simple origami-style move: a tote during the day or folded into an evening bag. Of the collection, Silvia Venturini Fendi said: "It's pure, simple, but complex", a statement that, of course, encapsulates the Fendi brand.

OPPOSITE Contrasting textures were seen in the Spring/Summer 2023 show.

OVERLEAF Layering of garments and exquisite technique were displayed in the dynamic Spring/Summer 2023 collection.

FENDI IN POPULAR CULTURE

FENDI ON SCREEN

**"The world of art has always been an
important aspect of our family life.
I grew up in our ateliers, places of energy,
of meeting, of discussion, where after sunset
actresses, directors and writers passed by"
– Silvia Venturini Fendi**

The Fendis' love and appreciation for the arts has always
been key to their creative process. Self-confessed
cinephiles, they began designing costumes for the
screen in the 1970s – from Italian productions such as
Visconti's *Conversation Piece* (1974), featuring actress Silvana
Mangano, to blockbusters like *Never Say Never Again* (1983),
directed by Irvin Kershner, with Barbara Carrera as Bond
Girl *Fatima Blush*. Fendi also dressed Michelle Pfeiffer in
Martin Scorsese's *The Age of Innocence* (1993), Madonna as Eva
Perón in Alan Parker's *Evita* (1996) and Gwyneth Paltrow as

OPPOSITE Gwyneth Paltrow wears a toffee-coloured demi buff
mink trench coat as Margot Tenenbaum in Wes Anderson's *The
Royal Tenenbaums* (2001). It was designed by Karen Patch and Fendi.

BELOW Madonna wore a Fendi light brown demi buff mink fur coat in *Evita*, 1996.

Margot Tenenbaum (sumptuous in a long, caramel-coloured mink coat) in Wes Anderson's *The Royal Tenenbaums* (2001). Designer Milena Canonero received the Best Costume Design Academy Award for her work on *The Grand Budapest Hotel* (2014), where actress Tilda Swinton's character Madame D wore a mink and hand-painted Fendi cloak. Patricia Field also received an Oscar nomination for her work in the fashion comedy drama *The Devil Wears Prada*. Here, Meryl Streep's character Miranda Priestly wore an unforgettable fitted short Fendi jacket, with a striking striped collar and cuffs. To celebrate their close bond with the world of cinema, from Italian classics to Hollywood sensations, an interactive exhibition called *Fendi Studios* took place in 2017, coinciding with Rome's International Film Festival.

Through the decades, Fendi has also made its way into popular culture through brand collaborations. Working with other fashion houses, artists and even technology, Fendi has temporarily reinvented and adapted its creative spirit to reach new audiences and fashionistas alike. When the Apple Watch was launched in 2015, for example, its new technology revolutionized the way we accessed our information – from emails to fitbits. With a detachable strap, the digital giant also partnered with several designers, including Fendi, to offer some classic strap designs to technophiles with a penchant for fashion, adding classic elegance to the futuristic watch.

In the music scene, hip-hop's Dapper Dan famously used "fake" customized Fendi fabric to dress his artists from the late 1980s and Kanye West made a statement when he shaved the venerated double F logo onto his head in 2006 before attending

ABOVE Meryl Streep wears a Fendi red Persian jacket with striped collar and cuffs in the acclaimed comedy drama *The Devil Wears Prada* (2006).

a Fendi party in Tokyo. Many other musical references include the Black Eyed Peas' 2005 hit "My Humps"; Child Rebel Soldier's "Don't Stop" in 2010; Chamillionaire's "Gucci & Fendi" in 2012 and Lady Gaga's song "Fashion" in 2013. Then, in 2018 (the year reality TV star Kylie Jenner was photographed in a tight Fendi *Zucca* dress, pushing her daughter in a matching Fendi pram), US rapper Nicki Minaj released the song "Chun-Li", from her fourth studio album *Queen*, where she rapped the lyrics "Fendi prints on". The single cover depicted a picture of herself, pin-up style, wearing a brown Fendi *Zucca* bomber jacket with matching vintage bikini bottoms. In a symbiotic relationship with the fashion house, this led to a collaboration (of 127 pieces) called, of

PREVIOUS Tilda Swinton pictured here wearing a hand-painted red silk velvet cloak embellished with black mink collar and cuffs in *The Grand Budapest Hotel* (2014), for which costume designer Milena Canonero won an Oscar for Best Costume Design.

RIGHT Kanye West attends a Fendi party in 2006 with the Fendi logo shaved into his hair, celebrating the launch of a new line of bags.

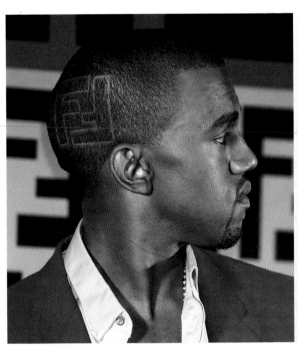

course, *Fendi Prints On*, which launched in 2019. It comprised a ready-to-wear capsule collection for women, men and children, and was heavily monogrammed. It included sports hoodies, lots of hot pink and silver in tight-fitting and cut-out dresses, logoed tights, high heels and caps. There were also some oversized rainbow branded aviators, swimwear, trainers, leggings and ski moonboots, as well as belt bags, and Baguettes in hot pink and silver. Some T-shirts and ties with pictures of Nicki also appeared in this bold collab, which featured a very slick LA poolside campaign, shot by Steven Klein.

Aside from the success of the superstar Baguette bag, Silvia Venturini Fendi designed the Peekaboo in 2008, for the Spring/Summer 2009 collection. This was a playful handbag that gets its name from the traditional children's game, and which very quickly rose to become a classic, joining the ranks of the most celebrated designs. Made in Tuscany by the best artisans, the leather bag was designed with a number of sections and a double closure, enabling it to be worn closed or left open to reveal its interior lining. In the designer's own words, this was "the only occasion in which a woman would be recommended to walk around with an unfastened and unlocked bag". This special bag, which exudes confidence, has become a big part of the brand's history, and has been made in many versions – some vertical, some horizontal and in a number of sizes (it comes in large, regular, mini and micro). Interesting partnerships have surrounded it too: in 2019, 10 years after it first came out, a campaign called #MeAndMyPeekaboo was launched, featuring a number of videos that focused on family values, each video starring a particular family with some of its members sharing intimate moments.

In the first episode, Silvia Venturini Fendi and her daughters Leonetta and Delfina candidly discuss each other ("My mum

is unstoppable, bossy woman, workaholic 100 per cent," says Leonetta; "She loves what she does," confirms Delfina) and they talk about their favourite Peekaboos. In another, Catherine Zeta-Jones and her daughter, Carys, are seen dancing in Rome with their respective bags. This campaign also included a short film, fronted by Kris Jenner, Kim Kardashian and her daughter North West (this was the five-year-old's fashion debut) and shot in Los Angeles. This time the film has a grainy Super 8 feel to it, as we witness three generations enjoying quality time together, bags in hand (including a mini version for North West). The house also invited visual artist Sarah Coleman, who resides in New York, to create some limited editions of the Peekaboo bag as part of the 2020 edition of Design Miami. And in 2022, model Adwoa Aboah starred in a campaign for the bag shot by Luca Guadagnino, where she floats over Rome – Tinkerbell-style – and descends by the stairs of the imposing Fendi headquarters.

OPPOSITE Kim Kardashian in a chocolate brown leather fitted dress from the Fendi x Skims collaboration.

RIGHT *Fendace* was a unique collection that fused the styles of Italian fashion houses Fendi and Versace.

For the Autumn/Winter 2020 catwalk, the bag was redesigned to appear more open, in a version called Peekaboo I See You, with interchangeable linings that you can match – either to your mood or to your outfit. The frame was also smaller and more structured, and was made in a number of finishes including a beautiful satin version with a Chevron pattern. Australian actress Naomi Watts fronted this #FendiPeekaboo episode, coinciding with the opening of the new Fendi Queen's Club flagship boutique in Sydney. The short promotional film, *Wild Untamed Naomi*, is a candid and light-hearted account of the actress spending time in her apartment, trying to relax and going through many emotions – some of which she releases by screaming, eating chocolate or dancing with her Peekaboo close by. In her own words, "I love the colours! And it is a classic shape that's very functional, whether you're travelling with it or just using it as a day-to-day bag. It just works."

LEFT Lila Grace Moss Hack walks the catwalk in a spectacular show hosted by both Versace and Fendi.

OPPOSITE Kate Moss walks the catwalk for the *Fendace* presentation, in a unique event that shook the fashion world.

Fendi Mania was the name of another collaboration, this time with heritage sports brand Fila, unveiled at Fendi's Autumn/Winter 2018. This capsule collection for men, women and children combined elements of '80s aesthetic with a luxury twist. An oversized logo designed by Scottish artist and Instagrammer Hey Reilly, who based it around the Fila font (in red and blue or white and yellow), was central to the look. It included mink coats, silk skirts and sportswear – heavily branded sweatshirts, hoodies, reversible bomber jackets, swimming costumes, jackets, skirts, tops and dresses. Accessories included shoes, boots and bags – bumbags and mini backpacks made with glazed coated canvas. Sports chic at its very best.

Another memorable capsule collection was launched in October 2021, this time with Kim Kardashian's shapewear company, SKIMS. Kim Jones came up with the idea when he noticed how much the Fendi team in Rome loved the shapewear brand, resulting in Fendi x SKIMS. This collaboration was inspired by archival sketches from a Lagerfeld collection dating back to 1979, and was an instant success (it was reported that the partnership generated an estimated US$3 million in sales within 10 minutes of its release). The ready-to-wear looks were co-designed by Kim Jones and Kim Kardashian West, and were based on figure-hugging sculpted silhouettes – from hosiery to leather dresses and puffer jackets. There was also some swimwear, logoed tights, bags in bright colours and some *Fendi First* mules, designed specifically for this limited edition.

Fendace was another highly anticipated and iconic fashion moment: instead of collaborating, Kim Jones (with Silvia Venturini Fendi) and Donatella Versace decided to exchange roles, trusting each other with their storied brands to create a unique perspective on them. "It's a swap rather than a collaboration and, most of all, it is done out of friendship," said Jones. This exchange resulted in the fabulous Fendi by Versace and Versace by Fendi collections for both men and women, which were presented at Milan, closing Fashion Week. The show began with 25 looks from Jones's collection: short dresses – some slashed, some held together by Versace's iconic gold safety pins; lots of baroque prints and gold chainmail garments, some floor-length evening looks and plenty of sky-high heels and gold jewellery. Kate Moss and Amber Valletta walked together to close this section. Then, while the backdrop changed from the Versace to the Fendi logo (a circular panel rotated to reveal the new branding), Donatella's 25 *Fendace* looks walked on. There was a lot of Zucca print in the traditional brown, and accents of bright colour, such as hot pink. Leopard prints, of course, made an appearance, as did some great denim looks. We also saw some stunning chainmail garments, such as minidresses with the Fendi logo printed onto the Oroton. Donatella also included sports caps with beautifully printed silk foulards around them – à la Audrey Hepburn in *Funny Face* (1957) – or worn as a bandana. The show was a huge success, with a stellar cast of models that included veterans such as Shalom Harlow, Karen Elson, Amber Valletta, Naomi Campbell and Kate Moss, as well as rising stars like Moss's daughter Lila Grace Moss Hack and American model Precious Lee. Demi Moore, Dua Lipa and Elizabeth Hurley, who wore *that* dress to the premiere of *Four Weddings and a Funeral* in 1994, were among the audience.

A beautifully polished campaign to accompany the presentation was shot by the great Steven Meisel, with an accompanying short film directed by Alex Maxwell. The film featured a nightclub with a glamorous bouncer at the door, complete with clipboard, asking for the code to get in. As the guests arrived, they had to say the password: that's right, "*Fendace*".

As a classic luxury brand, Fendi is often spotted at red carpet events. For Silvia Venturini Fendi their success lies in "high quality with a touch of irony and a surprise effect when talking about materials, it is never what it seems." The actor Jason Momoa turned up at the Oscars in 2019 wearing a pink blush velvet suit (with matching hair scrunchie) accompanied by his then wife, actress Lisa Bonet, in an exquisite Fendi couture dress. And the following year, singer Charlie Puth stole the limelight when he turned up in a yellow Fendi Autumn/Winter 2020 velvet tux to the Oscars' *Vanity Fair* afterparty.

LEFT Gwyneth Paltrow arrives for the 77th annual Golden Globe Awards, in a delicate, light brown Fendi sheer dress, 2020.

OPPOSITE Zoey Deutch wears a striking yellow Fendi gown to the 77th Annual Golden Globe Awards in Beverly Hills, California, 2020.

OVERLEAF A medium Fendi Baguette in brown leather with gold hardware.

When it comes to womenswear, Silvia maintains that, to make an impression, her outfits must observe Fendi's three Fs: "Femininity, fierce and a touch of fun." In 2022 US actress Barbie Ferreira wore a beautiful striped shoulder-less dress from the Studio 54-inspired Spring/Summer 22 collection to the Oscars afterparty, and Emma Watson selected a pretty Fendi grey sheer lace dress, which she also wore on Academy Awards night in 2023. Celebrities also love wearing Fendi off duty and plenty of them have been spotted in unmistakable looks, especially with the revival of the '90s logomania trend, and with the *Zucca* print making its way into streetwear.

RIGHT Jennifer Lopez carrying a Fendi bag, as seen in New York in 2018.

LEFT Rita Ora is spotted wearing Fendi at London's KISS FM studios.

Vintage is another trend that has enjoyed a comeback, and Fendi cult classics have been highly sought after in the preloved market – the boho-style Spy bag (designed in 2005 but currently not available) was recently worn by Rihanna, Tommy Dorfman and Bella Hadid. And the trend grows stronger as sister Gigi Hadid, Jennifer Lopez, Hilary Duff, Rita Ora and Cara Delevingne – and many more – are spotted when out and about wearing Fendi clothes and accessories, embodying timeless style, quality and, above all, the playful Fendi spirit.

INDEX

CREDITS

The publishers would like to thank the following sources for their kind permission to reproduce the pictures in this book.

Every effort has been made to acknowledge correctly and contact the source and/or copyright holder of each picture any unintentional errors or omissions will be corrected in future editions of this book.